Capriccios

Poems by

Pamela Martin

Capriccios
Copyright 2009 by Pamela Gowan

All rights reserved under International and Pan-American copyright conventions. No part of this book may be reproduced, stored in a retrieval system or transmitted in any form, electronic, mechanical, or by any other means, without written permission of the author.

International Standard Book Number: 978-0-578-02672-5

Illustrated by Kathleen Hardy.

Table of Contents

The Beginning

Promises to Keep 9
Mary, Queen of Scots 9
Dervish 9
A Freudian Slip 10
Epitaph 10
Ersatz Love? 10
Intoxication 11
Paean 12
Racecar Bob 12
An Interview 12
Talisman? 13
Prescience 14
The Love that Lasts and Lasts 14
Alice Roosevelt 14
Occupational Hazard 15
Frango Mints 16
Thanksgiving 16
March is a Charm 16
London Fog 17
Carpe Diem 18
Miss Alacrity 18
Solitude 18
A Weighty Matter 19
The Illiad and the Oddyssey 20
Purple Hearts 20
The Hamburger 20
Dehydration 21
A Great Dane 22
The Socratic Method 22
Rhyme of the Ancient Mariner 22
The Rape of the Lock 23
Arson 23
King Richard II 23
Clueless 24
Supply-Side Economics? 24
Edgar 24
"I Sing the Body Electric" 25
Wanderlust 25
A Sticky Situation 25
Guilt Trip 26
What Goes Up Must Come Down? 26
October 16th 26

The Fountain of Truth 27
Comic Relief 27
Hearing Voices 27
Post-Painterly Abstraction 28
The Mechanics of Writing 28
Awake! 28

The Middle

A Journey of a Thousand Miles 33
Lactose Free 33
Osculation 33
Crocodile Tears 34
Viola 34
Romanticism 34
Zoo Mass 35
Secular Humanism 36
Platitudes-a-Plenty 36
Free Will 36
Masonic Temple 37
The Eternal Present 38
A Night Mare 38
Keynesian Economics 38
Sanctuary 39
Bibliomania 40
Chastisements 40
Triage 40
The First Litterbugs 41
On the Brink 42
Selfish Gene 42
The Hanoverian Regression 42
"Give Peace a Chance" 43
American Realism 44
Stockholm syndrome 44
The W.C.T.U. 44
Heliocentrism 45
Dust Jackets 45
The Cooking Jean 45
Baccalaureate 46
De jure 46
Ethnic Cleansing 46
The Domestic Cat 47
NV 47
What Does Delaware? 47
Flockheart 48
Robin Hood 48

The End

The Vortex of History	53
A Complimentary Color	53
Strings Attached	53
"The Ghost of Christmas Past"	54
The Insouciant Gaul	54
"The Belle of Amherst"	54
Shortchanged	55
The Oedipus Complex	56
Plate Tectonics	56
Global Warming ☺	56
A Baker's Dozen	57
The Wisdom of the Ages	58
Horatio	58
Miss Demeanor	58
Ergophobia	58
Onomatopoeia: Silence	59
Taciturnity	60
Phaeton	60
Ah, Ha! *or* the "Ha Ha" Song	60
A Knack for Life	61
Beau Brummell	62
Circular Reasoning	62
The Key of Life	62
The War of Roses	63
The Individualist	64
"You had me at 'Hello'"	64
Performance Anxiety	64
Pirate's Plunder	65
"I Got a Vocabulary for Christmas"	66
Transubstantiation	66
Good Advice	66
"The Cha Cha"	67
Incidental Music	67
A Perfect Cadence	67
The Deadline	68
Dr. Seuss	68
Perhaps	68
Theology 101	69
No Pain, No Gain: "The Opium of the Masses"	70
"Police the Police"	70
Abstraction	70
P.H.D.	71
Diogenes of Sinope	71

The Beginning

Promises to Keep
Live!
Carpe Diem
Clueless
A Moral Dilemma

Promises to Keep

I am a pyromaniac.
I burn the midnight oil.
'Til 4:00 a.m. or later
On poetry I toil.
Now don't misunderstand me.
I do need my sleep.
But, like Robert Frost before me,
I have promises to keep.

Mary, Queen of Scots

Every living Anglophile
Will recognize the name
Of Mary, Queen of Scots,
Who lost her head upon the Nene.
It was her clear complicity
In a Catholic plot
That led just as ineluctably
To another Catholic plot.
Or was it rank simplicity
That finally did her in?
Being born of Henry's sister
Was her only sin.

Dervish

My jello is alive.
It jiggles just like me
And dances all around the bowl
Into an ecstasy!

A Freudian Slip

If I were Sigmund Fraud,
I would be afraid
Even in my wildest dreams
To call a spade a spade
Because you never know
What it will reveal
About your ego and your id
Although they are not real.

Epitaph

The world may never know
The person I have been,
The places I have been to,
The trouble I have seen.
But if it never knows me
The way I thought it should,
I know it knew me as it knew me.
It did the best it could.

Ersatz Love?

Everything's so fake these days,
Faux fur to costume jewels.
We use aspartame
Like Priscian uses rules.
But the one thing I can say
(The only thing that's real)
Is you and me together.
That's just how I feel.

Intoxication

The T.V. is my best friend.
It's with me all the time
Like a codependent lover
Or live-in concubine.
It greets me in the morning
And hasn't slept a wink.
It drains me of emotion
And will not let me think.

Paean

If I were born again,
It would be in Rye, New York.
There there'd never be
No politics or pork.
Everyone would love me.
I'd make quite a splash!
After all, it is the birthplace
Of my hero, Ogden Nash.

Racecar Bob

Bob is my favorite palindrome
But racecar works fine, too.
Racecar Bob and peppermint
Never make me blue.
Sometimes I get lonely
When he's not around.
But racecar Bob, as always,
Turns upside down my frown.

An Interview

An interview is a place to show
Everything you have come to know.
An interview is a place to tell
Everything you have done so well.
And interview is a place to shine,
A place to be so very refined.
An interview is a stressful thing
Where you must lie about everything.

Talisman?

There was a little ladybug
On the kitchen door.
I shooed it off with just one flick
But it held on as before.
So, I took a hammer from the drawer
(I could stand this bug no more)
And, after I banged down the door,
The bug began to soar.

Prescience

Science is another word
For every dogma you have heard.
Beaufort, Richter, Geiger, too,
Can measure everything but you.
And you we saved for the last.
Who but you could know the past?
He who knows the past, it's true,
Knows the future through and through.

The Love that Lasts and Lasts

The vicissitudes of life may change
But some things stay the same.
The way I feel about you,
The way I spell my name.
The mistakes I make that are my own,
The immutability of the past.
The end that's near and closing in,
The love that lasts and lasts.

Alice Roosevelt

Alice was a Roosevelt.
She lived in a grand style.
She had the best of everything
And yet she did not smile.
Her daddy bought her a Teddy bear,
Which was barely used.
She returned it unceremoniously
As if it were recused.
A character in her own right
Alice would always be.
"If you don't have anything nice to say,
Come sit next to me."

Occupational Hazard

If I could build a cottage
Made entirely of cheese,
Its value would increase with age
Like a Tasty Freeze.
But I could never leave my home
Out of fear and fear alone
That just one hungry Mickey Mouse
Could eat my cheesy home.

Frango Mints

Godiva was a lady
Who became a chocolatier.
Hershey was purveyor
Of hot cocoa and good cheer.
But neither could outmatch the man
Who I can more than hint
Makes my favorite chocolate candy
Marshall Field's Frango Mints.

Thanksgiving

I'm thankful for Thanksgiving Day.
So much so I have to say
I get down on my knees and pray
For proper gratitude.
My prayers were answered seven-fold
For seven weekdays I am told
That each is worth a pot of gold.
Now that's an attitude!

March is a Charm

A lucky, little leprechaun
Came to me and said:
"Weep not for dear St. Patrick.
Remember him instead
With festivities and shamrocks, too.
Dye the river green.
And treat him as you would in life,
As if he were Jim Beam."

London Fog

When I went to London,
I could see the air.
I wanted so to touch it
But I did not dare.
I packed my bags completely
And headed for the door
But thought it more discretely
To agonize some more.
After twenty years,
I still can see the air
But nothing in this world
To London can compare.

Carpe Diem

What lies in the future
Is a veiled mystery.
What lies in the past
Is a force of history.
But what lies in the present
Is a basic humanity
That imbues us with the spirit
To fulfill our destiny.

Miss Alacrity

Miss Alacrity always taught us
To always be on time,
That to do otherwise
Would be a heinous crime.
It's unkind, she told us,
To make somebody wait.
"Better late than never,
But better never late."

Solitude

Sometimes I think I think too much.
Sometimes I think I do.
The times I think I think too much
I think too much of you.
I think of what you said to me,
The things you used to say
And of the times you told me
You'd never go away.

A Weighty Matter

It snowed today and yesterday.
It is the Gospel truth
The artic age takes center stage
Here in cold Duluth.
It can be said that we'd be dead.
It doesn't take a sleuth
To come to know that all this snow
Could crush our sagging roof.

The Illiad and the Oddyssey

Homer wrote the Illiad
And the Oddyssey
Before he finished high school,
Although he could not see.
These are the facts of history
That compel us to believe
Anyone could do it
Unless we were deceived.

Purple Hearts

Purple is a regal color
Worn by kings and their lovers.
Bend your knee and soon discover
Who wears the pants.
For power is as power does.
Tread lightly, dear, just because
Colors fade and so it was
With our brief romance.

The Hamburger

McDonald's has sold billions.
White Castle sold a few.
Wendy's are old-fashioned.
Some are king-sized, too.
With or without French fries,
With or without cheese,
They're the world's fastest delicacy,
Pass the ketchup, please.

Dehydration

Every time I look around
I see a water tower.
Jumping out of nowhere
They multiply by the hour.
Some are painted with a smile.
Others just say, "THINK!"
Water tower, water tower everywhere
And not a drop to drink.

A Great Dane

Hamlet was a ham.
On this we can agree.
He avenged his father's murder
With verbal repartee.
No other son on earth
Could bring about such shame.
That's how Hamlet, Prince of Denmark,
Lost his royal claim.

The Socratic Method

When I ask a lot of questions,
My father says to me,
"Indeed, what is your problem?
You discombobulate me."
But when I ask a lot of questions
Surely he doth see
There is method to my madness,
And it's working palpably.

Rhyme of the Ancient Mariner

I'm so old I cannot see
Clearly what's in front of me.
But this albatross around my neck
Surely has been heaven sent.
For it has kept me out at sea
So long I got my G.E.D.
And that has left me free to roam
So far away but not alone.

The Rape of the Lock

I went to get a hair cut
But which one is unclear.
That joke's as old as Lincoln
Or older still I fear.
At least, there's one to tonsure.
At least, there's one to shear.
At least, there's one to snip off
If for a souvenir.

Arson

Prometheus gave us fire.
Venus gave us love.
We will never know
What they were thinking of.
As the flames of love enfold us
And burn within our hearts,
We can't help but notice
Cupid's little darts.

King Richard II

Here in Chicago
We have many traditions
Not the least of which
Are our rousing renditions
Of God save King Richard,
King Richard II!
He's only the sequel
But history beckoned.

Clueless

I live my life so fully
I haven't got the time
To comprehend the nature
Of the Great Divine.
Sometimes I think he's watching
But hasn't got a clue
About what we are doing
Or what we're going through.

Supply-Side Economics?

Tax and spend. Tax and spend.
It's the American way.
Tax and spend. Tax and spend.
There's no other way.
Tax and spend. Tax and spend.
It's the only way.
Spend and spend. Spend and spend.
That's what we do today.

Edgar

When I'm feeling useless,
I just think of you
And then I know the depths
Of what uselessness can do.
But are we all not useless
Writing poetry
That's as useless as the writing
On your Parnassian degree?

"I Sing the Body Electric"

To tell someone a story
Takes a special kind of skill.
To be a Faulkner or a Hemingway
Requires a force of will
Greater than a mustard seed
But smaller than a god.
Mostly it requires
That you become a lightening rod.

Wanderlust

I wonder as I wander
And I wander all the time
To the ancient pyramids,
Up the River Rhine.
When it is all over
As if by design
The whole of human history
Will, in fact, be mine.

A Sticky Situation

Tweety Bird and Donald Duck
Were selling contraband
To the innocents and children
Who were playing in the sand.
The dream police were called
And were arriving on the scene
Only to find that everyone
Was eating ice cream.

Guilt Trip

Whistler had his mother.
Abel had his Cain.
The wisdom of a lifetime
Was all they had to gain.
But if Whistler had been able
To raise a little cane,
Then surely his poor mother
Would be the one to blame.

What Goes Up Must Come Down?

I have the most indomitable of spirits.
Nothing brings me down.
Not the law of gravitation.
I'm the unsinkable Molly Brown!
Don't mind me for saying
It hasn't always been this way.
I learned to hold my own
And make the best of every day.

October 16th

Did you Noah Webster?
I think I knew one, too.
They say today's his birthday.
For all I know it's true.
He was a lexicographer.
By that I mean to say
Everyone should Noah Webster
On American Dictionary Day!

The Fountain of Truth

What better way to stay
Young, at least in heart,
Than to throw away your cares
And with circumspection part.
Misguided though you are,
Take my sage advice:
Do what you must do.
It's worth the sacrifice.

Comic Relief

Indigence and indolence
Usually come as a pair.
For them to be separate
Is really quite rare.
They feed on each other
Like fire and air.
And, in the end,
They're the cause of welfare.

Hearing Voices

This morning I picked out
An ensemble of clothes.
What I was thinking
Nobody knows.
But after I dressed
To my surprise
A voice started threatening
To 'out' my dress size.

Post-Painterly Abstraction

If I were naturalistic,
I'd paint "Snap the Whip"
With children running 'round and 'round
Careful not to trip.
But I'm a modern girl
And paint non-objectively
With my colors arbitrary
And my subject the abstract sea.

The Mechanics of Writing

I'm mechanical by nature.
I could make a bench
If only I could find
A left-handed monkey wrench.
But in my own defense,
As everybody knows,
Mechanical engineers
Write only turgid prose.

Awake!

The Irish celebrate the mystery
Of life after death
With a party in the memory
Of the mortal breadth.
They socialize with family
And greet their closest friends
And reflect upon God's mercy
And the life that never ends.

The Middle

One Hundred Poems
The Beauty of It All
Levitations
Myopia
American Realism
Parameters

A Journey of a Thousand Miles

How to start a poem.
How to start a play,
How to start a novel
When you don't have much to say.
How to start an engine
In the pouring rain.
How to start believing
In yourself again.

Lactose Free

The Cat in the Hat
Came to our house.
The first thing he did
Was frighten the mouse.
The next thing he did
Was corner the cow.
But as they say
He worships it now.

Osculation

It's a sign of affection
And a public display
Of the love that you give me
With each passing day.
It's the chance of a lifetime
In a lifetime of chance.
But more than anything
It's the soul of romance.

Crocodile Tears

Once upon the River Nile
I met a lonely crocodile
Who was so sad he could not smile
Not even to pretend.
But that was, oh, so long ago.
I hate to say I told you so.
Depressions come. Depressions go.
And now he is my friend.

Viola

She played me like a violin,
A Stradivarius.
She played so well that I could tell
She was a true genius.
She played by heart her solo part
With methodology
And taught me all I need to know
Of musicology.

Romanticism

Give me the old world.
Give me parfait.
Give me a map
Of the Appian Way.
Give me the life
My father once knew.
Give me the hope
This dream will come true.

Zoo Mass

I went on a safari
To the Serengeti Plain.
I would have liked it better
If it wasn't for the rain.
The wildlife there was awesome
Like a visit to a zoo
Or a quiet little soiree
At a certain party school.

Secular Humanism

Life is but a master seed
That grows into a tender reed.
But like the gentle, fragile flower
It dies a little every hour.
Yet life moves forward as we speak
Flowing from the ancient Greeks.
It matters not what life is.
What matters is that we have lived.

Platitudes-a-Plenty

Heart of hearts, I love the well.
I love you more than words can tell.
I love you more than you love me.
I love you for what you can be.
I love you, heart, for you are mine
And will stand the test of time.
Heart of hearts, I say to you
To myself I must be true.

Free Will

They did their best to cleanse the air
Of misery and God's despair
But only made us more aware
That we must set the goal.
We emerged triumphantly
Stronger now that we can see
There exists the possibility
Of freedom of the soul.

Masonic Temple

Brick by brick, they tell you,
Build it they will come.
Make it high and mighty.
Second best to none.
And when you are finished
It will last and last,
A constant reminder
Of the greatness of the past.

The Eternal Present

We are in the moment.
In the here and now,
Living free and easy
Making it somehow.
Life goes on without us.
Be that as it may.
There's really nothing wrong
With living for today.

A Night Mare

My flashlight is so tiny.
It hardly makes a light.
What will I do
In the middle of the night?
Fumble around blindly
Missing every mark
Or simply get a horse
That can see in the dark?

Keynesian Economics

I have the wisdom of Solomon
And the patience of Job
And a highly developed
Temporal lobe.
But the one thing I don't have,
I don't have a job.
And right now my prospects
Seem quite macabre.

Sanctuary

Some people find great solace
In the bosom of the Church.
Other people find real comfort
In the swaying of a birch.
I prefer the birch myself
Because it is so strong
Although the history of the Church
Is so very long.

Bibliomania

A classic is the kind of book
That you have to read.
A mystery is the kind of book
About a dreadful deed.
A romance is the kind of book
That you love to love.
A thriller is the kind of book
That's all of the above.

Chastisements

The corporal kind of punishment
Is a passing fad
Reserved only for miscreants
Who've been very bad.
Tine outs can be useful
If you have the time
But do not underestimate
The benefits of whine.

Triage

When I get up in the morning,
The first thing that I do
Is feed my little kitties
And have a drink or two.
The last thing I remember
Before I close my eyes
Is how much I get done
When I prioritize.

The First Litterbugs

Hansel and Gretel
Made it O.K.
To leave all your crap
And be on your way.
One man's detritus
Is another man's flan.
The best you can do
Is catch-as-catch-can.

On the Brink

He took her to the precipice.
She had been before.
He told her it was just a cliff.
The rain began to pour.
He reached out and took her hand
And called, "Sweet, Emily."
The Belle of Amherst spoke at last:
"Death is mine enemy."

Selfish Gene

In a solipsistic universe
There is only me.
In this lonely world
You could never be.
Narcissism is a kind
Of selfish chemistry
That isolates the spirit
From its sociality.

The Hanoverian Regression

George succeeded Edward.
Elizabeth succeeded George.
At least they all spoke English
Since the time of Valley Forge.
We are now much wiser
And can truly say
We speak the *King's* English
To this very day.

"Give Peace a Chance"

He entered old Jerusalem
On a donkey's back.
When it came to free publicity,
They said he had a knack.
We celebrate the miracle
Of his Virgin birth.
All he ever wanted
Was to establish peace on earth.

American Realism

Abraham was honest,
Honest to a fault.
But never did he ever
"Enter" Mrs. Galt.
No matter what he did,
He couldn't tell a lie.
That is how we know
He ate that cherry pie.

Stockholm syndrome

I and my captor
Are one and the same.
When I was captured,
I didn't complain.
No longer a captive
I wouldn't go home.
Without my captor
I feel alone.

The W.C.T.U.

The experiment was noble.
(The results decidedly not.)
We drank so much whiskey
Our teeth began to rot.
And when it was over,
The country was besot,
Which is why this experiment
Was almost forgot.

Heliocentrism

Every waking minute
Of every waking hour
I look to the sun
To give me the power
To live my life
As I see fit
And to make
The most of it.

Dust Jackets

The things that we hold on to
Are the things we can't let go.
We hold on to them anyway
Because we need to know
That we are part of something
That is larger than ourselves
And will not be forgotten
Like tomes upon the shelves.

The Cooking Jean

When it comes to cooking,
Mostly I do not.
I like my food served
Either cold or hot.
Teach a man to fish
And he'll eat for life
But most of the time
He prefers a wife.

Baccalaureate

The liberal artist works the hardest
Just to get ahead.
I should know for I must go
And earn my daily bread.
Very often we will soften
As we mop the floor.
But deep inside we have our pride.
We are the working poor.

De jure

In a litigious society
We love to go to court.
We love to sue our neighbors.
We have our favorite tort.
In a lawless society,
It's a free-for-all.
It's each man for himself
Like one big booty call.

Ethnic Cleansing

When Irish eyes are smiling,
It's because they are.
When they go to school,
You know they will go far.
So much for the Irish.
They are very clean
Wandering through the world
Selling Irish Spring.

The Domestic Cat

They say cats are curious
But are they very smart?
I say they are for just today
I compiled a chart
Of the things they can do.
(They can do a lot)
But, when it comes to household chores,
Mostly they cannot.

NV

"I want what you want,
And I want it now,"
The covetous woman
Said with a bow.
"I want what you have,"
She said with a glean,
"Next door the grass
Is always so green."

What Does Delaware?

The tiny state of Delaware
Has so much to give.
Despite its size it's still the place
Where many people live.
The museums and the gardens
Grace this "first" of states
But they're really just a front
For corporation gates.

Flockheart

Mother was a goose.
Father told us so.
It was a family secret
Only he would know.
So, when you cook your goose,
Remember our dear mother.
We still miss her so
Especially little brother.

Robin Hood

I take from the rich
And give to the poor
Because, as they say,
The poor need it more.
But a poverty of imagination
Can't be restored
Which is why education
Can't be ignored.

The End

The Twelfth Book of Mischief
A Baker's Dozen
Silence: The epic
A Knack for Life
Sweet Sixteen
Periphrasis: or the Art of Circumlocution
A Beautiful Mind
Lemons into Lemonade

The Vortex of History

They say it's a circle.
(Some say it's not)
Or a straight line
Made up of dots.
I say it's a gyre
Spinning around
As it gently
Slides on the ground.

A Complimentary Color

Fishing for a compliment
Is as old as time.
They say self-deprecation
Is more potent than fine wine
If it can elicit
A kind word or two
That can make the difference
When you're feeling blue.

Strings Attached

Would you believe when I was ten
(As much as I remember then)
I played second fiddle
As I danced around the griddle.
Now I play the first violin
In Symphony Center for Gwendolyn.
Out of the frying pan into the fire.
But, frankly, I prefer the lyre.

"The Ghost of Christmas Past"

September babies are Christmas presents.
Just count back nine months.
I'm September 20th.
I am not a dunce.
Mom and dad were active
Under the mistletoe.
I should know 'cuz I was there
Twenty years ago.

The Insouciant Gaul

The Frenchman labels everything
With a carefree guile.
You can't say it. You can't spell it.
Go that extra mile.
I admire from afar
Their perfume and their food.
They perfected everything
Especially the nude.

"The Belle of Amherst"

Death to her was gripping.
It almost was alive.
It was her one obsession.
It helped her to survive.
She had short but sweet encounters
With other subjects, too.
God knows, in her place and time
There was nothing else to do.

Shortchanged

We each live on an island
Separated at birth.
Yet we are loosely tethered
Enjoying the warm hearth.
If there was a reason
We were put on earth,
I do not believe
He got his money's worth.

The Oedipus Complex

Who wants to solve the riddle,
The riddle of the Sphinx?
"I do," said poor Oedipus,
"I know what he thinks."
A man must kill his father
If he will be king
And satisfy his mother
With all worldly things.

Plate Tectonics

The Geological Survey
Knows a thing or two
About this ever-changing world
That's shifting under you.
Continental drifts
Are causing us great grief
Making mountains out of mole hills
And creating the Barrier Reef.

Global Warming ☺

I'm so old I can remember
How cold it was in December.
That's why I had a special coat
That was so big it made me float.
But I liked it just the same,
So much so, I can't complain.
I no longer need it not.
It is so warm. I like it hot.

A Baker's Dozen

"Muy caliente! Muy caliente!"
Is what the baker said.
I know this much is certain
He makes a real fine bread.
In his measuring system
A "dozen" is thirteen.
Even a trixadecaphobe
Knows that's what he means.

The Wisdom of the Ages

History is liberation
From the tenets of the past.
Each day is a new day
When you're free at last.
But, if it is nonbinding,
What is it good for?
It goes without saying
There is no forevermore.

Horatio

It's rude to be crude and lewd to be nude.
But you ought to know,
"There is nothing either bad or good
But thinking makes it so."

Miss Demeanor

When they were giving out "Looks,"
I thought they said, "Books."
I said, "Give me a creature feature."
That's what I got, and I like it a lot.
Now I am a teacher.

Ergophobia

I often wander down the path
Of the conditional clause.
What if I had married
Mr. Santa Claus?
Would it make me happy
Working half a year
Or would I still be sitting
Crying in my beer?

Onomatopoeia: Silence*

*It goes without saying.

Taciturnity

Religion, sex and politics
Are subjects taboo
To Pamela Martin
Although sometimes I do
Need a diversion
From the usual fare.
But I do not relish them.
I use them with care.

Phaeton

I am photophobic.
I can't stand the light.
In the brightest hour
I want only night.
It's as if poor Helios,
(Greek god of the sun),
Lost his sense of humor
And his only son.

Ah, Ha! *or* The "Ha Ha" Song

Ha ha ha ha ha ha ha,
Ha ha ha ha ha.
Ha ha ha ha ha ha ha,
Ha ha ha ha ha.
Ha ha ha ha ha ha ha,
Ha ha ha ha ha,
Ha ha ha ha ha ha ha,
Ha ha ha ha ha.

A Knack for Life

I have a knack for living
And a knack for life,
A knack for anything
That doesn't cause strife.
A knack for you
And a knack for me,
A knack for celebrating
History.

Beau Brummell

You are the most beautiful
Person in my eyes.
Then why is it you put on
That wonderful disguise?
Think about the energy
You put into your stealth.
Are you hiding from someone
Or hiding from yourself?

Circular Reasoning

The dialog inside my head
Spits out vitriol
Faster than a speeding bullet
I cannot control.
The alpha and omega
Take a leaping bound.
This vertiginous circle
Just keeps spinning 'round.

The Key of Life

It seems to me this symphony
Is comprised of cacophonous sounds.
Despite its tonal harmony,
Dissonance abounds.
To modulate to another key
They use a "pivot" chord
That transposes everything
Like chalk on a chalkboard.

The War of Roses

We have an English garden
That grows as wild as rice.
Not a topiary.
It isn't quite as nice.
The French manicure their spaces
To the "nth" degree.
Laid back are the English
Like a cup of tea.

The Individualist

I am but
A wordy gnome
Who turns a phrase
And writes a poem.
If you like
What I have done,
You may be
The only one.

"You had me at 'Hello'"

"Guten tag! Guten Tag!"
The German says to you.
"Aloha!" and "Shalom!"
Say the Hawaiian and the Jew.
But I have to say
(And this my profession),
You only get one chance
To make a first impression.

Performance Anxiety

Did you ever see a square dance
Or a patriot act?
I have seen them with both eyes,
And it is a fact
That neither is edifying
Nor particularly enlightening
But both can be terrifying
And especially frightening.

Pirate's Plunder

I feel I plagiarize
Every word I write.
Are they mine to utter
Or do I laconically recite
The one who first spoke them
At the beginning of time?
I simply abuse them
To make this silly rhyme.

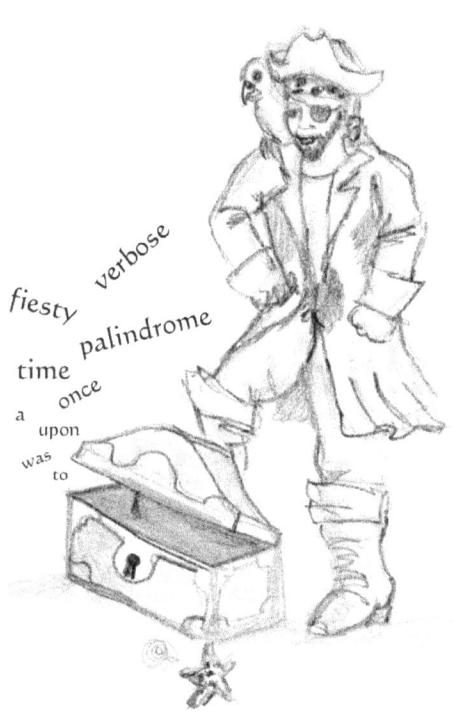

"I Got a Vocabulary for Christmas"

A "juggernaut" is
An irrepressible force
Used to denote
A going off course.
I use it glibly
But I don't really know
What a juggernaut is.
I hope it don't show.

Transubstantiation

Sometimes mamma goes
To the ballet dance
Where she leads a life
Of beauty and romance.
But when it's all over
She's well aware
The life she lives
Cannot compare.

Good Advice

"In order to kill time,
Work it to death,"
My father told me
In his final breath.
When advice is not taken
(Although it is free),
You'll be mistaken
Regrettably.

"The Cha Cha"

One, two,
Cha-cha-cha.
Three, four,
Cha-cha-cha.
Five, six,
Cha-cha-cha.
Seven, eight,
Cha-cha-cha.

(Repeat)

Incidental Music

Bollywood is Hollywood
In another place.
On the Indian continent
It is a saving grace.
With or without warning,
They burst into song.
But we do not mind.
We sing right along.

A Perfect Cadence

Sometimes I wonder
If my feet touch the ground.
Why do I march
To that rhythmic sound?
The beat of the drummer
Steadies my soul.
To reach the stars
Makes my drum roll.

The Deadline

It's always hanging
Over your head.
It's not for nothing
They call it "dead."
Infinitely wise,
It annihilates
Any man or woman
Who hesitates.

Dr. Seuss

They say I know
Thing One and Two
More than I
Should say or do.
If I did not,
I tell them this:
If I did not,
I'd be remiss.

Perhaps

Evil forces lurk about
In every nook and cranny.
Within the darkness of my soul
I think it's uncanny.
We lead lives of turpitude
And unabashed indifference.
Can a man of probity
Really make a difference?

Theology 101

"Medina's Temple"

It only takes one Muslim
To ruin it for the rest.
But I don't think the Muslims
Should be put to the test.
Theirs is a religion
Based on the sanctity
Of Mohammad's teachings.
I could never be.

"Jesus was a Jew: The Historical Christ"

It only takes one Jew
To ruin it for the rest.
But I don't think the Jews
Should be put to the test.
Theirs is a religion
Based on history.
I'm a *novis homo*.
I could never be.

"The catholic Catholic Church"

It only takes one Catholic
To ruin it for the rest.
But I don't think the Catholics
Should be put to the test.
Theirs is a religion
Based on mystery
Literally and figuratively.
I could never be.

"The Light at the End of the Tunnel"

It only takes one "Puritan"
To ruin it for the rest.
But I don't think the Puritans
Should be put to the test.
Theirs is a religion
Based on charity.
Emphatically and eternally,
I will always be.

No Pain, No Gain: "The Opium of the Masses"

When the night has gone
And the light of day
Come peeking through the clouds
That melt along the way,
You begin to feel
The glimmerings of pain
Of love and loss and lethargy
And all that does remain.

"Police the Police"

Some police are like people
Who prey on the poor.
Nobody stops them.
That would cause war.
But this odious behavior
Cannot be ignored
Until social justice
Again is restored.

Abstraction

The parietal, occipital
And temporal lobes
Are filled with synapses
And tiny microbes.
But it is the frontal
That gives us center.
It is our teacher
And tormentor.

P.H.D.

This is my dissertation
Piled High and Deep.
It caused me so much agony
I could hardly sleep.
But now that it's all over
I can rest assured
Knowing my valiant efforts
Went completely unobserved.

Diogenes of Sinope

If I do sound cynical,
It's because I am.
Jaded and arch critical,
I now understand
Innocence is not something
That can linger on.
It's always in the past tense.
It is now long gone.

Other books by Pamela Martin Available on **amazon.com**:

American Realism
A Beautiful Mind
The Beauty of It All
A Knack for Life
Lemons into Lemonade
Levitations
MYOPIA
Periphrasis: or the Art of Circumlocution
Silence: The epic
Sweet Sixteen
The Twelfth Book of Mischief/ A Baker's Dozen (dual anthology)

www.ingramcontent.com/pod-product-compliance
Lightning Source LLC
LaVergne TN
LVHW011430080426
835512LV00005B/357